# WEDDING FASHIONS
## 1862–1912

*380 Costume Designs from "La Mode Illustrée"*

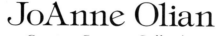

EDITED AND WITH
AN INTRODUCTION BY

### JoAnne Olian

*Curator, Costume Collection*
MUSEUM OF THE CITY OF NEW YORK

DOVER PUBLICATIONS, INC.
*New York*

Published in Canada by General Publishing Company, Ltd., 30 Lesmill Road, Don Mills, Toronto, Ontario.
Published in the United Kingdom by Constable and Company, Ltd., 3 The Lanchesters, 162–164 Fulham Palace Road, London W6 9ER.

## Bibliographical Note

*Wedding Fashions, 1862–1912: 380 Costume Designs from "La Mode Illustrée"* is a new work, first published by Dover Publications, Inc., in 1994.

## Library of Congress Cataloging-in-Publication Data

Wedding fashions, 1862–1912 : 380 costume designs from La mode illustrée / edited with an introduction by JoAnne Olian.
    p.    cm.
  ISBN 0-486-27882-4 (pbk.)
    1. Wedding costume—France—History—19th century.   2. Wedding costume—France—History—20th century.   3. Mode illustrée.   I. Olian, JoAnne.
GT1753. F8W43  1994
392′.54—dc20                                                        94-11479
                                                                          CIP

Manufactured in the United States of America
Dover Publications, Inc., 31 East 2nd Street, Mineola, N.Y. 11501

# Introduction

THE IDEALS OF domesticity and connubial bliss reached their apotheosis in the nineteenth century. Promoted in England by Queen Victoria, and embraced with equal ardor on the Continent and in America, the family was the raison d'être of the nineteenth-century woman, and marriage her path to fulfillment.

While the late eighteenth century, particularly in France, had been a time of liberation for women, when divorce was permissible and participation in political affairs was encouraged, after Napoleon divorce was abolished and the nineteenth-century glorification of marriage as an ideal moral state began to evolve. At the end of the century, as women began to attend college and work outside of their homes, there was again a resurgence of female emancipation, but the prevailing attitude remained:

> Contentment does not come from careers . . . If those single women who have done the best work in their respective arts, should tell the truth, they would declare that they knew they would have been happier married and the mother of children. That is woman's natural career and an unhappy married woman is a freak. So is a woman with a career. Both are outside of what God and Nature intended them to be. (Lillian Bell, 1906)

The nineteenth-century woman reflected the prevailing Romantic climate, a recreation of a mythical, idyllic time when knights performed courageous acts of chivalry for their delicate, helpless ladies. A woman's need to be protected and cherished was proclaimed by such eminent figures as Honoré de Balzac, who said we should believe in marriage as in the immortality of the soul. Since women had few legal rights, this attitude served a practical purpose by charging the male sex, viewed as superior mentally and emotionally as well as physically, with responsibility for the fairer—and weaker—sex.

By the 1840s, the Romantic mood had blossomed into Victorian sentimentality mirrored in the cozy, middle-class domesticity of the English monarch and her growing family. At first as simple in its outward manifestations as Victoria's unadorned white satin wedding gown, its embellishments became increasingly elaborate. Home, marriage and family were a tightly woven tapestry replete with flowers and curlicues, whose needlework equivalent appeared in every magazine of the period and decorated the overstuffed, heavily curtained interiors that provided a haven from the world outside.

From early childhood little girls played bride and dressed their dolls in wedding finery. The realization of a girl's most fervent wish was marriage, hence her wedding marked the most important rite of passage in her life. Its trappings were of the utmost

importance and the planning of such an auspicious occasion occupied much of her time and daydreams. Romance was a blend of the intangible, symbolized by the future husband, and the tangible, consisting of trousseau, wedding, honeymoon and home. Many of the bridal customs and trimmings in fashion today made their first appearance in the nineteenth century, when they were described enthusiastically in numerous magazines such as La Mode Illustrée, which catered to women's dreams. One contemporary weekly, The Illustrated American, commented:

> Weddings and bridal rehearsals, luncheons, dinners, and parties, are . . . regarded as the most important functions of the year, more concern centering around the paraphernalia of a bride-elect than about the finest frocks worn by unattached girls or safely settled matrons. From her silk hosiery and high-heeled white slippers to the blossoms or tiara supporting her veil, each word regarding the affianced lady is read with avidity by the multitude. For the instant every woman is more or less idealized by her attitude in entering matrimony. She is a momentary heroine. . . .

Young men were educated to take their place in a public society and for them this meant college and possibly the law or medicine. However, higher education was not crucial to a young woman, whose ultimate goal was marriage. Her principal focus was on preparation for her future role as housewife and consort. Aside from a superficial (and obligatory) smattering of culture which included the ability to play an instrument, to sketch and to sprinkle a few foreign phrases in conversation, her education emphasized etiquette and, more important, the management of a household and children, with or without benefit of servants.

The first prerequisite was a suitable husband, and there were numerous opportunities to meet members of the opposite sex. In addition to introductions by family and friends, social occasions such as skating parties and dances abounded. Debutante balls, called bals blancs in France, at which eligible young men and white-clad young women danced under the watchful eye of chaperons, ensured that young people of the same social milieu would have opportunities to meet.

When a couple fell in love, it was customary for the young man to ask the girl's parents for their permission to wed. In France, if the parents agreed, the boy's parents then presented a formal proposal to the parents of the girl and a dinner was held at the home of the bride-to-be. This signified an official engagement and her fiancé presented her with a ring. During this period the families negotiated the dowry and fixed a date to sign the contract, which took place before a notary in the presence of friends and relatives. In Paris it was to become fashionable for the reception to be held on the night of the contract signing instead of the day of the church wedding, and by 1900 this was firmly established as the date of the nuptial festivities, occasioning *La Mode Illustrée* plates depicting appropriate garb. Typically, the contract dress was low-necked with elbow-length sleeves and was as formal as a dinner dress. It could be in any shade fashionable at the time.

In America, while there might be informal discussions regarding financial settlements on the engaged couple, the attitude was one of embarrassment, which, according to *Vogue's Book of Etiquette,*

> the men of the family feel . . . more than any one else. If it were a question of one savage to another, with so many head of cattle against six sheep and a pony, it would be easy. But to arrange with a co-parent in embryo what he will give his son and meet it, generously or cautiously, with what we shall give our daughter, and to settle where and how those young people can live on it is just as troublesome when the other person is a friend as when he is a perfect stranger.

There was no formalized acknowledgment of legalities and American wedding ceremonies customarily took place immediately preceding the celebratory breakfast or luncheon.

Once an appropriate mate was found and the engagement solemnized, the next order of the day was the trousseau, which included personal as well as household linen in quantities as lavish as the family's wealth would permit. A modest trousseau might consist of three dozen of everything while a generous one, each piece of which was usually monogrammed, could be counted by the gross. Alphabet styles suitable for embroidering were a regular feature of *La Mode Illustrée*'s bridal issue. In France the bridegroom-to-be sent his fiancée a *corbeille* on the day the contract was signed. Originally a basket, its contents might be equivalent in value to a year's salary. It was heaped with traditional gifts such as new or heirloom lace, jewelry, furs and trinkets such as fans and candy boxes. A prayer book to be carried during the wedding ceremony and a purse filled with new gold coins were always included. Even the future Empress Eugénie was not above accepting such gifts, and received in addition 30 boxes of textiles from the enterprising silk manufacturers of Lyons, to be made into costumes for her trousseau.

In 1851, underwear was not considered a topic for discussion. *Les Modes Parisiennes*, reporting the display of a trousseau, asked, "Have these displays not their danger? Should a mother allow her daughter to see them?" However, it soon became customary for both trousseau and *corbeille* to be exhibited before the wedding as mute testimony to the social and financial position of the family. As late as 1885 magazines routinely described the contents of the trousseaux and *corbeilles* of socially prominent brides, but by 1891 it had ceased to be good form:

> The custom of exhibiting the *corbeille* and the gifts sent to the bride by her relatives and friends, this custom, in strongly questionable taste—has completely fallen into disuse among people of true refinement. The display of intimate lingerie was painful for the fiancé, and shocking to the modesty of more than one fiancée. Besides, there was a parvenu ostentation in such display.

In addition, trousseau lingerie, originally piled up in impressive numbers sufficient for the remainder of a young bride's life, became subject to the vagaries of fashion, and by the end of the century would no longer be purchased in quantities to last a lifetime. In a 1927 *Vogue* article, a bride told a friend:

> Mother asserts that trousseaux are out of date, anyhow most impractical. Grandmama Carrol once told me she had twenty-four dozen of everything given her when she was married. Fashions in those days didn't change as often as they do now, so brides took no chances. Granny actually showed me handkerchiefs that were part of her trousseau, which she, however, never uses now. Why not? Because of their being huge squares of linen. She nowadays has the daintiest of chiffon "hankies," some of them flowered, while others look like rainbows. Why certainly, Granny is very much up to date!

Groom and attendants merely serving as background, the cloud of satin and tulle that was the bride was the undisputed star of the wedding. By mid-century, her dress was definitively white and impossible to confuse with any other type of formal attire. The sumptuous and heavy fabrics, the high-necked bodice, the train, the orange-blossom trim, the bouquet, were all part of the strict social ritual of marriage. Dress was never more clearly one of the most visible signs of "correctness" and "suitability" so valued by nineteenth-century society, than in the bridal gown. While wedding dresses were subject to the same metamorphoses of silhouette as all fashionable dress, they differed from them because of the traditions surrounding this ceremony. White, historically the color of chastity, has been de rigueur for almost every ceremony for females, including Confirmation, graduation and debut, but it was not ubiquitous for weddings until early in the nineteenth century, when it was worn by bride and bridesmaids alike. Not until the 1880s did the attendants dress in color. In 1883, *Demorest's Monthly Magazine* commented:

> Quite a new departure has been taken recently in the adoption of colors for the dresses of bridesmaids instead of the repetition of the conventional white. Why it should have ever been considered necessary for bridesmaids to wear white does not appear. There is a pretty sentiment in the purity of the robes of the bride, but the bridesmaids ought to be differentiated in some way from their companion who is about to take a serious step, and separate herself forever from the old happy life. It ought to represent the innocence and joyousness of youth, the free hopeful spirit which is still theirs, and which would naturally express itself in tints and colors, in light delicate green, mauve, pink, and dull pale gold.

In another issue, *Demorest's* advocated a different color for each bridesmaid. Alice Roosevelt, the daughter of President Theodore Roosevelt, avoided the issue at her wedding by eliminating bridesmaids entirely.

Almost without exception, white was worn for a first marriage, unless the ceremony was very informal, in which case the bride might be married in her going-away clothes. Unlike garb for other rites of passage, nuptial magnificence was not limited by custom or taste. Not any white would do, admonished the *Ladies' Home Journal* in 1894:

> When wearing a white gown thought must be given to the becomingness of the shade, for, after all, there are as many tints in white as in other colors; the one that may suit the pale blond is absolutely unbecoming to the rosy brunette. Dead white, which has a glint of blue about it, is seldom becoming to any one. It brings out the imperfections of the complexion, tends to deaden the gloss of the hair, and dulls the brightness of the eyes. The white that touches on the cream or coffee shade is undoubtedly the most artistic and best suited to the general woman. However, in choosing it one must be careful not to get too deep a tone, which is apt to look not quite dainty, and to give the impression of a faded yellow, rather than a cream white.

Velvet, heavy satin, brocades and huge quantities of embroidery, lace and tulle were deployed in the service of the bride. Paradoxically, jewelry was frowned on, and only a gift from the groom, such as a strand of pearls or a simple piece of jewelry, was acceptable.

The years from 1860 to 1912 witnessed enormous fashion changes, all of which were echoed in bridal toilettes. At first, the crinoline held out the enormously full skirts of wedding dresses measuring five yards around at the hem, which gradually flattened in front and bunched up in the back until they formed a bustle in the 1870s. By 1880 the bride was encased in an unyielding hourglass-shaped bodice and pencil-slim skirt that gave way to a revival of the bustle in the mid eighties. In 1890, the back fullness deflated and the yardage was transformed into a skirt that flared at the hem. Emphasis shifted to the sleeve, which looked increasingly like the melon or leg-of-mutton it was often called. By the turn of the century, fullness shifted to the derrière, a result of the S-shaped corset that thrust the top half of the body forward in a matronly monobosom effect while the lower half stuck out prominently behind. Gradually the torso regained its verticality, due to the corsets which created an Empire line, a revival of the Neoclassical silhouette popularized by the Empress Joséphine 100 years earlier. From 1900, the neck was completely swathed in a wide band of lace or tulle. The veil completely covered the hair, framing the face, and a minimum of trim became fashionable, creating an effect of chaste, almost nunlike simplicity. By 1912, the exotic influence of Paul Poiret, the leading couturier in Paris, was apparent even in the simplest harem-skirted wedding dress.

Fabrics, from sumptuous satin to filmy mousseline de soie, also followed the current mode, with heavier materials preferred until the latter years of the nineteenth century, when they were replaced by lighter-weight satins and chiffons suitable to the simpler fashions of the twentieth.

In spite of its seeming sartorial extravagance, the wedding gown often appeared again in another incarnation. During the nineteenth century, most dresses were made with separate bodices and skirts, and when the fabric was especially sumptuous, sometimes one skirt would serve both a matching décolleté bodice suitable for a ball and a sleeved bodice appropriate for dinner or receptions. Wedding gowns often did double duty afterward, minus any strictly bridal trim such as orange blossoms. In Edith Wharton's *The Age of Innocence,* when newlywed May Archer asks her husband what to wear to a reception, he suggests her wedding dress. She cries, "If I only had it here! But it's gone to Paris to be made over for next winter, and Worth hasn't sent it back." In one of the myriad books of etiquette published at the turn of the century, the writer cautioned, "The wedding dress answers for an evening gown for three months, but if it is trimmed with orange blossoms they must be replaced by white roses or other flowers. Worth and Paquin always put a parure of white roses in the box with the wedding frock."

The pages of *La Mode Illustrée* are filled with suggestions for remaking wedding dresses into costumes for visiting, receptions and balls. Most of the directions require sending the dress to be dyed, and one issue recommends several types of silk for the dress, including Duchesse satin, peau de soie and crepe de chine because of their ability to accept dye. Another idea was simply to cover the original dress completely in tulle or lace, stating, "The effect cannot be but the prettiest, the richest and the most elegant."

The honeymoon, or wedding trip, was also covered at great length by the arbiters of manners. Since its avowed purpose was to ensure a couple's privacy, the 1886 *Livre du Mariage* recommended that the newlyweds travel with trunks containing everything necessary to "create a charming environment for themselves wherever they might go." Mrs. Burton Kingsland advised, "The bride's travelling costume should be quiet and inconspicuous, that her new condition may not be advertised to every stranger." Favored destinations were Niagara Falls and the Italian lakes. However, on their lengthy honeymoon, the Newland Archers eschewed Italy for Paris, where May spent a month with the best dressmakers, followed by July in Interlaken and Grindelwald, and August at Etretat on the Normandy coast, ending their trip with a two-week stay in London where the groom ordered *his* clothes. Over a half-century later, Amy Vanderbilt was to write that the modern honeymoon is much simpler, and usually much shorter. She noted, "My mother's lasted three months and included a trip on horseback through part of the Rockies. In the 1860s a honeymoon could encompass a whole summer and might include the entire wedding party—at the bridegroom's expense." With such strenuous itineraries it is not surprising that in 1873 *Harper's Bazar* described a sturdy "traveling dress added to spring trousseaux, and which serves usually for 'second best' street suit, . . . a polonaise with simply trimmed skirt of camel's hair serge. . . ."

Today's honeymoon may have to be postponed until bride and groom, often both busy with careers, can coordinate their schedules so that they can run off together to some remote spot which was probably undiscovered or inaccessible when *La Mode Illustrée* was published. The workaday uniform of today's bride is the practical, functional tailored suit, doffed on weekends and holidays for more relaxed garb such as T-shirt and jeans. Informality has become the byword of fashion and very few occasions require dressing up. As a result, entrance-making ensembles have become irrelevant and the couture is vanishing. Its spectacular style, exquisite fabrics, cut and workmanship and, most important, exorbitant cost, have rendered its clothing vulgar and démodé to contemporary eyes. However, when confronted with the bride-to-be, the current de-emphasis on fashion comes to an abrupt halt.

From the 1960s to the mid-1970s, weddings were definitely out of fashion. Since then the trend has been toward increasingly lavish events. Hardly makeshift affairs, theme weddings, requiring months of planning, are popular. *Gone with the Wind* is a perennial favorite, while Disneyworld and Universal Studios in Florida are currently the scene of innumerable nuptials. In 1992, 2.5 million weddings took place in the United States, at an average cost of $15,800. The total added up to $32 billion which was spent on everything from invitations to honeymoon luggage, and encompassed such items as wedding gifts and furnishings for the newlyweds' first home, in addition to the cost of the actual event. Stationers, florists, photographers, jewelers, manufacturers of silver and china, caterers, limousine services and airlines are a few of the industries sharing in the bonanza.

A visit to any newsstand or bookstore reveals innumerable magazines and glossy coffee-table books devoted to every aspect of weddings, from cake to honeymoon. Bridal-gift registries, considered old-fashioned and crassly materialistic a short time ago, are proliferating. Caterers vie to create romantic and original settings to lure prospective brides and grooms and it is not unusual for the couple, or the bride's parents, to go into hock to pay for the big day. A glance at any one of the myriad magazines devoted solely to weddings reveals countless pages of advertising by china, glassware and silver manufacturers, hotels and airlines, in addition to companies specializing in gowns for the bride and her attendants, accounting for the thickness and numbers of bridal literature.

The tremendous variety of wedding dresses are a marvel of creativity and eclecticism, especially when they are generally limited in color to traditional white. No limits, however, are placed on the imagination of the designer, for whom every period in history provides inspiration. The Renaissance, the eighteenth century and both the First and Second Empire in France vie with the antebellum South in popularity. Even the baker has a chance to show his skill in the *pièce montée,* developed in the late sixteenth century when sugar was first refined, now enjoying a revival. A sculpted sugar wedding cake can cost as much as the bride's dress, especially when designed to repeat its theme.

Traditionally the pièce de résistance of a designer's collection, as well as its predictable and popular finale, is the wedding dress. No contemporary fashion editor would dream of diminishing its glamour by suggesting ways to recycle wedding finery by dyeing a dress or taking it apart and remaking it. The last refuge of extravagant romanticism, it incorporates the sense of drama and fantasy possible only on this occasion. The floating, full-skirted, trained, fairy-tale costume is the embodiment of a dream, realized by the white-clad bride as she glides down the aisle to the strains of Mendelssohn on this most auspicious of days, the radiant cynosure of all eyes . . . a momentary heroine.

JoAnne Olian
*New York City*
*February 1994*

Bride's coiffure.

LEFT: Dress of white antique moire, the skirt with a demitrain. The hem, 4 m. 80 cm. in width (app. 5 yds.), is trimmed with three double-headed puffs, lightly gathered. The bodice is high-necked, straight and belted. A puff simulating a square bertha is applied to the bodice. The mid-length sleeves are trimmed with puffs. The belt has long streamers edged with a narrow, slightly darker, band of moire. The veil is of tulle. RIGHT: Dress of white organdy. The skirt is trimmed with three flounces of lace, each edged with a pinked white taffeta ruche. The bodice is high-necked, trimmed in front with the same ruche. The sleeves are slit at the seam, with a ribbon bow placed at the top of the opening. The veil is of tulle.

Matinee of white mousseline (of silk, cotton or wool—sheer, soft and
supple) from Magasins du Louvre, rue de Rivoli.

Outfit for seaside or travel from Mme Vignon, rue de Rivoli. (This outfit would be equally suitable for a going-away suit.) Ecru mohair overskirt gathered up to reveal a matching petticoat with a narrow pleated border, and trimmed with wide and narrow black velvet bands. The overskirt is trimmed like the petticoat, with only a single band of black velvet. It is caught up at intervals with appliqué motifs of violet cashmere piped in black velvet. The bodice is in the guardsman style; the coattails, lined in violet cashmere, are turned back; the revers, the sleeves and the padded *bourrelets* (shoulder rolls) are also of violet cashmere with black velvet trim. White piqué vestee. White mousseline cravat with black velvet bow.

Bride's toilette. LEFT: Dress of white taffeta trimmed with a lace flounce. A white taffeta ribbon ruche edges the lace all around. The high-necked bodice is trimmed in front with a narrow ribbon ruche. A bouquet of orange blossoms is held by the belt, with wide streamers. Mid-length sleeves, slit, trimmed to match the dress. Large veil of white tulle. RIGHT: Dress of brilliant blue taffeta. The skirt is edged with a narrow, finely pleated ruffle of black taffeta, surmounted by black velvet ribbons and white yarn appliquéd at right angles. The trim is repeated on the bodice, the sleeves and the belt, which has long streamers, tied in front. White crepe hat, embroidered in white chenille, with white feathers.

Bridal toilettes from Maison de la Commission Générale, rue d'Hauteville. LEFT: White mousseline, trimmed with two pleated flounces, topped with a double flounce. Pointed waist, buttoned bodice, long sleeves; large tulle veil, framed by two white taffeta rouleaux. RIGHT: White antique moire, edged with a matching finely pleated flounce at the hem. The applied scroll motifs on the skirt, sleeves and bodice are of white taffeta ribbon ruche; a similar ruche frames the pointed waist. This ruche is lightly gathered in the center. Headdress of jasmine and orange blossoms; matching bouquet at waist: undersleeves of white tulle with white taffeta cuffs. White gloves; white poult-de-soie boots.

Toilettes from Mme Castel-Bréant, rue de Sainte-Anne. LEFT: White poult-de-soie dress, trimmed with a wide lace flounce surmounted by a rouleau trimmed with pearls; lace-trimmed overdress of white mousseline in princesse style; long white tulle veil. RIGHT: White taffeta dress with a wide fringe topped with white silk cording at the hem; white lace crisscrosses to form squares bordered with fringe. Belted bodice; narrow sleeves, trimmed with crisscrossed white lace; long white tulle veil.

Toilettes by Mme Fladry, rue du Faubourg-Poissonière. LEFT: Toilette for the mother of the bride. Matching dress and paletot in wet-sand poult-de-soie. The trim is composed of a band of white poult-de-soie embroidered with black pearls. The paletot is trimmed with black lace. White hat of puffed tulle adorned with sprigs of holly. MIDDLE: Sister of the bride. Mauve taffeta dress striped in a deeper shade of mauve; saw-tooth edged hem with a band of mauve taffeta simulating a petticoat. Matching paletot. White hat of puffed tulle with dracaena leaves and white beaded flowers. RIGHT: Bride. White satin underdress; overdress completely shirred and puffed with a garland of orange blossoms above the bottom tier; matching flower cluster at waist and on each shoulder. Long white tulle veil.

Brides' costumes from Mme Rossignon, rue Laffitte. LEFT: White satin dress, trimmed with white taffeta piping and pearl buttons, simulated underskirt, Marie-Antoinette fichu of white lace; white tulle veil; orange-blossom coronet. MIDDLE: Dress with double skirt in repped silk. The overdress and hanging sleeves are edged with white fringe and satin; the veil is silk tulle. RIGHT: White taffeta dress with bands of white velvet simulating a second skirt; hanging sleeves of white lace match the lace that trims the velvet. White chenille fringe; white tulle veil.

Toilettes by Mme Fladry, rue du Faubourg-Poissonnière. LEFT TO
RIGHT: Suit for 5-to-7-year-old girl. Wedding dress of polished
organdy. Wedding dress of mousseline. Satin wedding dress.

Wedding outfits and town suits by Mme Fladry.

Brides' toilettes by Mme Fladry, rue Richer. LEFT TO RIGHT: Toilette of faye (soft, light fabric with silk warp and wool weft or fill) for the younger sister of the bride. White satin toilette. Suit for 2-to-4-year-old girl. Suit of dark wood color. Toilette of white faye.

Models by Mme Fladry, rue Richer. LEFT TO RIGHT: Bride's toilette in faye. Two-tone foulard dress. White satin wedding dress. Girl of 10 to 12. White repped silk bridal toilette.

Bridal toilettes by Mme Fladry, rue Richer. LEFT TO RIGHT: Under-dress of white faye trimmed with pleated ruffles; matching tablier and bodice, or tablier and bodice of white Indian cashmere; bows of white faye ribbon; white tulle veil; wreath of orange blossoms. Dark blue faye petticoat trimmed with matching puffs and ruche; tunic and bodice of dark blue damask; faye sleeves. White faye skirt; tunic of white mousseline with Valenciennes lace. Dress of faye in a medium reseda green, bodice in a deeper shade of the same color; shirred and puffed sleeves of smooth white crepe. Underskirt of white taffeta or sateen, skirt and tunic of white mousseline with pleated ruffles of the same mousseline and white taffeta piping; ribbon bows of white taffeta; sprays of orange blossoms.

Brides' toilettes. LEFT: White satin. RIGHT: White faye.

Linen and lingerie from Magasins du Louvre. *Fig. a:* Embroidered insertion. *Fig. b:* Nightdress. *Fig. c:* Trim of a nightdress. *Fig. d:* Scalloped nightdress. *Fig. e:* Shirt of striped toile. *Fig. f:* Collar. *Fig. g:* Cuff. *Fig. h:* Nightcap. *Fig. i:* Man's collar. *Fig. j:* Man's cuff. *Fig.*

*k:* Camisole. *Fig. l:* Man's nightshirt. *Fig. m:* Wrapper, front and back views. *Fig. n:* Camisole. *Fig. o:* Woman's underdrawers. *Fig. p:* Nightcap. *Fig. q:* Embroidered edging. *Fig. r:* Lace edging. *Fig. s:* Petticoat.

Linen and lingerie from Magasins du Louvre. *Fig. a:* Part of a nightdress. *Fig. b:* Nightgown with insertion. *Fig. c:* Collar. *Fig. d:* Nightgown. *Fig. e:* Embroidered insertion. *Fig. f:* Man's collar. *Fig. g:* Cuff. *Fig. h:* Collar. *Figs. i & j:* Nightcaps. *Fig. k:* Percale shirt. *Fig. l:* Petticoat. *Fig. m:* Nainsook wrapper, front and back views. *Fig. n:* Peignoir for hairdressing. *Fig. o:* Low-necked chemise. *Fig. p:* Man's underpants. *Fig. q:* Woman's underdrawers.

Various toilettes by Mme Fladry, rue Richer. LEFT TO RIGHT: Dress of faye and armure (front view). Dress of faye. Bride's toilette. Dress of faye and armure (back view).

Brides' toilettes by Mme Fladry, rue Richer. LEFT TO RIGHT: Back and front views of toilette of white mousseline. Toilette of foulard and mousseline. Toilette in faye.

Wedding toilettes from Mme Coussinet, formerly Maison Fladry, rue Richer. LEFT TO RIGHT: Sister of the bride. Bride's toilette. Little sister of the bride. Bride's toilette. Mother of the bride.

Wedding toilettes from Mme Fladry-Coussinet, rue Richer. LEFT TO RIGHT: Mother of the bride, dress of bronze faye. Bride, dress of faye. Sister of the bride, dress of faye and silk jardinière. Bride, dress of white silk brocade and plain silk. Little sister of the bride (5-to-7-year-old child).

From Mme Delaunay, rue Godot-de-Mauroy. LEFT TO RIGHT: Bride's dress. Dress of surah. Satin dress.

From Mme Coussinet, rue Richer. LEFT: Bride's toilette. Round skirt of white satin adorned at the hem with two matching puffs. The skirt is almost completely covered with three rows of white chenille fringe, each strand ending with a white pearl bead. High-necked bodice of brocaded white satin, cutaway style in front, long train in back. Long, narrow sleeves edged with lace at wrists. Neck ruff and jabot of the same lace. Tulle illusion veil falling only to the waist in front, and in back to the end of the train, which is edged with a double pleated ruche of plain white satin. RIGHT: Sister of the bride. Dress of pale gray merveilleux satin. The hem flounce is topped by a torsade of amethyst velvet. Riding-habit bodice of amethyst velvet, with gray satin facing and revers. Hat of gray plush with large ombré feathers in shades of amethyst.

Bride's toilette.

From Mme Coussinet, rue Richer. LEFT TO RIGHT: Bride's dress of moire. Satin dress. Bride's dress of voile.

From Mme Senet, rue du Quatre Septembre. Bride's toilette with lace
veil arranged in mantilla fashion. CENTER: Costume jewelry.

From Mme Delaunay, rue Godot-de-Mauroy. LEFT TO RIGHT: Reception toilette of satin (back). Bride's toilette in duchesse satin. Dress for little girl of 5 to 7 years of age. Toilette for young lady.

From Mme Coussinet, rue Richer. LEFT TO RIGHT: Ball toilette. Ball gown of striped gauze.
Bride's toilette. Dinner toilette.

From Mme Coussinet, rue Richer. LEFT TO RIGHT: Ball toilette of tulle. Toilette for 10-year-old girl. Toilette of flowered satin. Mantelet of cut velvet. Bride's toilette. Ball toilette of silk gauze.

Brides' toilettes from Mme Coussinet, rue Richer.

Wedding toilettes from Mme Coussinet, rue Richer.

Underwear and wrappers from the Grands Magasins du Louvre. *Fig. a:* Nightcap. *Figs. b & c:* Camisoles for ladies and young girls. *Fig. d:* Nightcap. *Fig. e:* Lady's drawers. *Fig. f:* Chemise. *Fig. g:* Lady's drawers. *Fig. h:* Combing sacque, back and front views. *Fig. i:* Printed woolen matinée. *Fig. j:* Plastron and cuff. *Fig. k:* Matinée with crocheted trim.

LEFT: Wrapper of flecked plush. RIGHT: Wrapper of wool twill.

Wedding toilettes from Mme Coussinet, rue Richer.

Bride's coiffure by M. Camille, rue du Quatre Septembre.

Bride's toilette from Mme Coussinet, rue Richer.

Bride's toilette from Mme Coussinet, rue Richer.

From Mme Coussinet, rue Richer. Left: Mother of the bride or groom. Right: Bridesmaid.

From Mme Coussinet, rue Richer. LEFT: Two brides' toilettes. RIGHT, TOP: Bridesmaid. RIGHT, BOTTOM: Wedding toilette for a widow.

TOP: *Fig. a:* Orange-blossom spray for hair. *Fig. b:* Epaulet of orange blossoms. *Fig. c:* Spray of China asters and butterflies. *Fig. d:* Hair ornament. *Fig. e:* Wreath of Ceres. *Figs. f–i:* Bridal slippers. BOTTOM: Wedding toilettes from Mme Coussinet, rue Richer. OPPOSITE, TOP: Bride's coiffure by M. Camille, rue du Quatre Septembre.

TOP: Bride's coiffure and ball coiffure, by Maison Camille, rue du Quatre Septembre. BOTTOM: Models by Mmes Coussinet-Piret, rue Richer. LEFT TO RIGHT: Toilette for little bridesmaid. Toilette for the

mother of the bride. Bride's toilette. Toilette for young bridesmaid.
BOTTOM, RIGHT: Hat for a bridesmaid from Maison Nouvelle , rue de
la Paix.

Lingerie from Magasins du Louvre. *Fig. a:* Embroidered drawers with side closing and embroidery. *Fig. b:* Night sacque. *Fig. c:* Night sacque with lace insertions. *Fig. d:* Collar of stitched English lace. *Fig. e:* Drawers with wide yoke and closed drawers. *Fig. f:* Chemises with elegant and simple trim. *Fig. g:* Nightcap. *Fig. h:* Morning cap. *Fig. i:* Camisole with side closing. *Fig. j:* Simple night sacque. From Mlle de la Torchère, rue de Rennes. *Fig. k:* Combing sacque, morning cap. *Fig. l:* Matinee in batiste.

From Mlle de la Torchère, rue de Rennes. LEFT, TOP: Matinee in foulard. LEFT, BOTTOM: Matinee in crepe. RIGHT: From Mmes Coussinet-Piret, rue Richer. Elegant dressing gown.

*Fig. a:* Bride's coiffure by M. Camille, rue du Quatre Septembre. From Mmes Coussinet-Piret, rue Richer: *Fig. b:* Mother of the bride. *Fig. c:* Bride's toilette. *Fig. d:* Dress for a girl of 8 to 9. *Fig. e:* Dress for little girl of 5 to 7. *Fig. f:* Dress for silver anniversary. *Fig. g:* Dress for a bridesmaid of 13 to 14. *Fig. h:* Bride's toilette. *Fig. i:* Formal toilette for young matron. *Fig. j:* Back view of fig. h. *Fig. k:* Back view of fig. i.

f

g

h

i

j

k

From Mmes Coussinet-Piret, rue Richer. LEFT TO RIGHT: Little bridesmaid of 11 to 12. Reception toilette. Bridesmaid of 14 to 15. Dinner toilette. Bride's toilette of satin and silk mousseline.

*a*

*b*                    *c*

*Fig. a:* Bridal toilette from Mme Sauveur, rue du Cherche-Midi.
From Mlle Louise Piret, rue Richer: *Fig. b:* Toilette for the mother of
the bride. *Fig. c:* Bride's toilette. *Fig. d:* Outfit for best man. *Fig. e:*
Toilette for bridesmaid. *Fig. f:* Bridal toilette from Mme Angenault,
rue de Provence. *Figs. g & h:* Brides' coiffures by Maison Camille.

d        e

g

f

h

LEFT TO RIGHT: Toilette for bridesmaid. Toilette for a young married
wedding guest.

From Mmes Guermont et Bonnefoy, rue de Provence. LEFT TO RIGHT: Toilette for mother of the bride, the skirt of silver-gray taffeta. Bridesmaid's toilette, for a little girl, of finely pleated pink crepe de chine, trimmed with insertions of cream guipure. Bride's crepe de chine toilette, the trained skirt arranged in stitched pleats ending above the hem to allow for more fullness. The trim is composed of a draped mousseline fichu edged with lace and ending on the left side under a spray of orange blossoms. The tulle veil is fastened by a diadem of orange blossoms. Bridesmaid's toilette of pale blue diagonally pleated louisine.

Lingerie patterns. *Fig. a:* Nightshirt. *Fig. b:* Shirt. *Fig. c:* Drawers for boy. *Fig. d:* Chemise. *Fig. e:* Night sacque. *Fig. f:* Drawers for girls. *Fig. g:* Corset. *Fig. h:* Combination for ladies and girls. *Fig. i:* Corset cover. *Fig. j:* Shirt. *Fig. k:* Nightshirt. *Fig. l:* Drawers for gentleman.

*Figs. m & n:* Night sacques for ladies. *Figs. o & p:* Ladies' chemises. *Figs. q & r:* Ladies' drawers. Border of initials for table linen, sheets, towels, etc.

Brides' coiffures from Maison Camille, rue du Quatre Septembre.

Bridal toilette from Mme Blanche Limousin, rue La Fayette. Ivory crepe de chine, trimmed with mousseline de soie of the same shade, shirred with small headings. A tulle veil and a garland of orange blossoms finish the toilette. INSET: Bridal coiffure by Maison Camille, rue du Quatre Septembre. Back view of bridal toilette.

Bridal toilette by Mmes Guermont et Bonnefoy, rue de Provence.

Bride's toilette of duchesse satin by Mlle Louise Piret, rue Richer. This very becoming, simple toilette is executed in ivory duchesse satin; the long-trained skirt, fashioned in nine gores, is without trim. The pointed and draped bodice is made with a shirred mousseline de soie yoke, framed front and back by a lace fichu. The bouffant satin sleeves have a lace ruffle above deep mousseline cuffs. A tiny bouquet of orange blossoms is placed on the front of the bodice. The toilette is completed by a large tulle veil draped on top of the head and held by a small diadem of orange blossoms.

Bridal toilette in supple satin, by Mlle Louise Piret, rue Richer. The trained skirt is trimmed at the hem with two groups of pleats, each surmounted with a mousseline de soie ruching. The skirt has a tablier of lace. The bolero, edged with two wide pleats, exposes a draped waistline. The mousseline de soie yoke is closed by small white velvet bows and framed by two pleats, on which are superimposed a band of shirred lace. The mid-length sleeves, lightly draped, are edged with a lace ruffle. The toilette is completed by a tulle veil held by a cluster of orange blossoms.

Bridal toilette by Mlle Louise Piret, rue Richer. The skirt of this toilette, executed in white silk crepe de chine, is shirred at the sides and back of the waistline; the tablier is framed by two unpressed pleats widening toward the hem. The skirt is trimmed near the hem with a band of shirred mousseline framed by two puffs with small headings. The shirred bodice is mounted on a yoke of cream guipure fashioned in a point and trimmed with puffs similar to the ones on the skirt. The short bodice reveals a corselet-belt of Liberty satin. The half-length sleeves, ending in lace ruffles, are encircled by puffs.

Empire style wedding dress by Mlle Louise Piret, rue Richer. This toilette of supple satin is trimmed at the hem with three lace flounces, ending at the train on each side. These flounces are held at intervals by tiny clusters of orange blossoms. The dress is mounted on a plastron of tucked mousseline de soie and adorned with a bolero of guipure; the half-length sleeves end in lace ruffles held by guipure armbands.

a

b

f g

h i

c d e

From Mme Blanche Limousin, rue La Fayette. BACK ROW: *Fig. a:* Toilette for young matron in the wedding party. *Fig. b:* Bridesmaid's toilette. FRONT ROW: *Fig. c:* Elegant suit for boy of 8 to 10. *Fig. d:* Lace-trimmed bridal toilette. *Fig. e:* Supple taffeta toilette for the mother of the bride. *Fig. f:* Rear view of fig. a. *Fig. g:* Rear view of fig. b. *Fig. h:* Rear view of fig. d. *Fig. i:* Rear view of fig. e.

Models by Mlle Louis Piret, rue Richer. LEFT TO RIGHT: Bridesmaid's or party toilette for young lady of 15 to 17. Elegant Empire-style dress for 8-to-10-year-old girl. Bridesmaid's toilette. Princesse dress for the evening of the contract signing. TOP: Rear views of the fashions.

LEFT: Matinee and skirt of lawn. RIGHT: Elegant lace-trimmed peignoir.

Summer lingerie. *Fig. a:* Empire matinee in nainsook with tucked yoke. *Fig. b:* Square-necked nightdress of lawn trimmed with insertions of Valenciennes simulating a bolero; pagoda sleeves edged with ruffles, trimmed like the top of the chemise. *Fig. c:* Chemise and underdrawers set for a young lady in nainsook with embroidered trim; the neckline and the drawers have scalloped edges. *Fig. d:* Elegant set consisting of a lace-trimmed batiste Empire chemise and drawers; yoke has embroidered insertions threaded with ribbon; drawers edged with a ruffle and trimmed with Valenciennes lace. *Fig.*

*e:* Corset cover and petticoat of nainsook, trimmed with tiny tucks and lace and edged with embroidery. *Fig. f:* Chemise and drawers set trimmed with tucks and lace insertions; this set matches fig. b. *Fig. g:* Short-sleeved Empire nightdress of fine batiste, with lace insertions and ribbon trim. *Fig. h:* Nainsook petticoat edged with a deep flounce adorned with groups of tucks and broderie anglaise. *Fig. i:* Nightdress of lawn mounted on an Empire bolero trimmed with embroidery and lace insertions.

LEFT: Bride's toilette of ivory mousseline de soie trimmed with garlands of ''bride's bouquet'' roses and greens. The draped bodice, framing a tucked mousseline yoke with a high collar, crosses in front and is held by a spray of orange blossoms. The sleeves consist of several ruffles. A tulle veil attached under a wreath of roses completes the toilette. RIGHT: Bride's toilette in supple silk. The skirt is arranged in an inverted pleat on each side. A wide lace insertion is placed above the hem. The bloused bodice and the corselet-belt of draped Liberty silk are mounted on a lace yoke. The bouffant sleeves end in two lace ruffles. The veil, shirred to form a puffed heading, is attached to a diadem of orange blossoms.

LEFT: Ball toilette by Mlle Louise Piret, rue Richer. CENTER: Bridal coiffure by Maison Heng, rue Bergère. RIGHT: Princesse-style bridal toilette by Mlle Goery, rue Littré. This toilette is of white Liberty satin trimmed with lace and tulle. The bodice is draped lightly above the waist and held by shoulder straps of satin with Valenciennes insertions. The bodice, high collar and long, extremely tight sleeves are of pleated tulle lined with mousseline de soie. The toilette is finished by a tulle veil attached at each side of the chignon under a spray of orange blossoms.

From Mlle Louise Piret, rue Richer. LEFT TO RIGHT: Toilette for wedding guest. (Rear view, left, top.) Toilette for the mother of the bride of pale heliotrope mousseline de soie trimmed with lace dyed to match and slightly darker inserts. The skirt is composed of lace panels. The edges of the tunic are adorned with a wide lace insertion of a slightly deeper shade. The bodice reveals a guimpe of pleated white tulle with long sleeves. The draped sash is of ribbon. (Rear view, left, center.) Bridesmaid's toilette: The skirt is of hydrangea crepe de chine arranged in groups of pleats. The bodice and sleeves are entirely covered in Valenciennes. A Liberty satin scarf serves as belt. (Rear view, left, bottom.)

LEFT: Bride's toilette of ivory crepe de chine, draped at the waist and held by a mother-of-pearl buckle; shoulder straps continue down the skirt, ending in silk fringe in a scarf effect. The bodice, of tucked crepe de chine, has a low round neck over a guimpe with long, shirred tulle sleeves trimmed with tiny satin buttons on the seam. (Rear view, right, top.) RIGHT: Bride's toilette in silk voile. (Rear view, right, bottom.)

*h*     *i*

*a*

*j*     *k*

*b*

*c*     *d*

*Fig. a:* Dress for bridesmaid. *Fig. b:* Dress for young matron in the wedding party. *Fig. c:* Toilette for bridesmaid by Mlle Goery, rue Littré. *Fig. d:* Bridal toilette in brocaded satin from Mlle Piret, rue Richer. *Fig. e:* Bridal toilette in mousseline de soie by Mlles Sauveur de la Torchère, rue du Cherche-Midi. *Fig. f:* Toilette for the mother of

e

f

l

m

g

the bride by Mlle Piret, rue Richer. *Fig. g:* Toilette for wedding guest from Mlle Goery, rue Littré. *Fig. h:* Rear view of fig. c. *Fig. i:* Rear view of fig. d. *Fig. j:* Rear view of fig. a. *Fig. k:* Rear view of fig. b. *Fig. l:* Rear view of fig. e. *Fig. m:* Rear view of fig. f.

Fig. a: Toilette for bridesmaid from Mlle Goery, rue Littré. *Fig. b:* Bride's coiffure by Maison Heng, rue Bergère. *Fig. c:* Bride's toilette by Mlles Sauveur de la Torchère, rue du Cherche-Midi. *Fig. d:* Ball coiffure for young matron. *Fig. e:* Ball coiffure for young lady. Both styles by Maison Heng, rue Bergère.

Models from Mlle Louise Piret, rue Richer. LEFT: Bride's toilette
with draped skirt. RIGHT: Bride's toilette in *météore*.

*Fig. a:* Toilette for civil ceremony. *Fig. b:* Bride's toilette in *météore* by Mlle Piret, rue Richer. *Fig. c:* Elegant toilette. *Fig. d:* Toilette for bridesmaid. *Fig. e:* Bride's toilette with lace blouse, from Mlle Goery, rue Littré. *Fig. f:* Toilette for the mother of the bride. *Figs. g & h:* Hats

d

e

f

h

l

m

n

for wedding guests by Mme Colombin, rue de la Tour d'Auvergne.
*Fig. i:* Rear view of fig. a. *Fig j:* Rear view of fig. b. *Fig. k:* Rear view of
fig. c. *Fig. l:* Rear view of fig. d. *Fig. m:* Rear view of fig. e. *Fig. n:*
Rear view of fig f.

LEFT: Bride's toilette of crepe de chine (rear view to left). RIGHT: Bride's toilette of Liberty satin (rear view to right).

Bride's toilette from Mlles Sauveur de la Torchère, rue du Cherche-Midi.

BOTTOM, LEFT TO RIGHT: Bridal toilette in crepe de chine with Liberty satin belt and bands on skirt and sleeves; a garland of orange blossoms seen through the tulle veil completes the coiffure. Bridal toilette in Liberty satin and mousseline de soie trimmed with white guipure; the satin skirt is partially hidden by a mousseline de soie tunic edged with a narrow border of guipure which also forms the tight cuffs, yoke and high collar; a bouquet of orange blossoms fastens the satin belt; the veil, draped over a low coiffure, is held by a garland of flowers. Dress for the mother of the bride, to be made in velvet of a deep shade such as green, plum or black; the yoke, with high collar, is made of gold tulle lined with mousseline de soie; jet braid edges the bodice and cuffs and catches the draped skirt. TOP, LEFT TO RIGHT: Rear views of the toilettes.

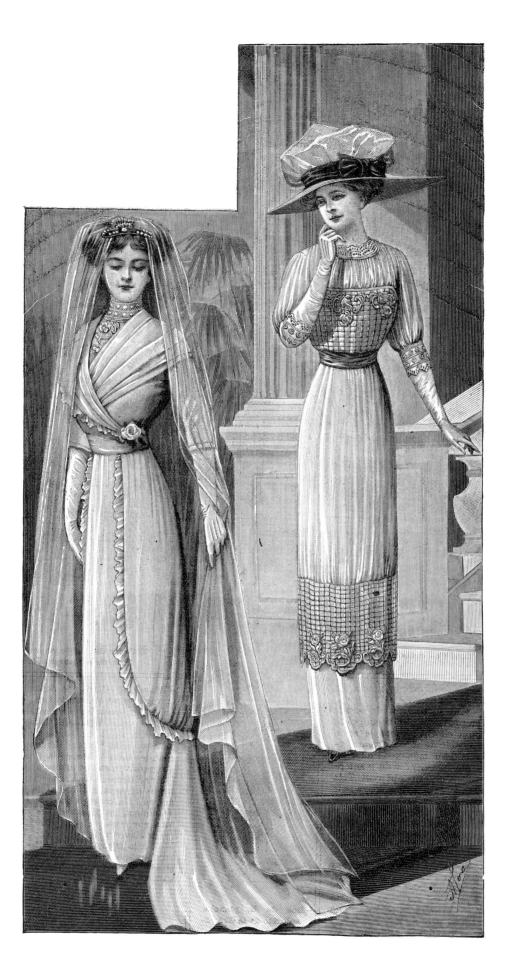

LEFT: Bridal toilette with draped bodice by Mlles Sauveur de la Torchère, rue du Cherche-Midi. The skirt consists of a tablier cut in one piece with the flounce longer in the back to form a square train. The bodice opens over a lace plastron with high collar framed by draped tulle crossing in front to form a fichu. The half-length sleeves are of silk covered with tulle. (Rear view at left.) RIGHT: Toilette for bridesmaid from Mlle Goery, rue Littré. Made in chalk white silk voile trimmed with heavily applied silver thread. The shirred bodice has a scoop neckline trimmed with antique embroidery, which also forms the cuffs of the shirred sleeves. (Rear view at right.)

LEFT: Toilette for elderly wedding guest. Black etamine trimmed with Liberty satin and lined in black silk. (Rear view, right, top.) RIGHT: Toilette for the mother of the bride. Leather-color mousseline de soie partially covered with a tunic of black Chantilly lace. The bodice crosses in front, over a plastron with high collar of white mousseline de soie which also forms the sleeve cuffs. (Rear view, right, bottom.)

From Mlle Piret, rue Richer. LEFT TO RIGHT: Fashionable bridal toilette of ivory Liberty silk with Irish lace insertions. Bridesmaid's dress of pale blue silk mousseline over embroidered white linen. Simple bridal toilette of white charmeuse.

Models by Maison Piret, transferred to Maison Maria, rue Royale.
LEFT: Wedding dress of *météore* (rear view, left, top). RIGHT: Bridal
toilette with guipure trim (rear view, left, bottom).

Contract toilette by Mlle Goery, rue Gerbillon (rear view at left).

*Fig. a:* Lace-trimmed bride's toilette by Mlle Piret, rue Richer. *Fig. b:* Rear view of fig. a. *Fig. c:* Bridesmaid's toilette by Mlles Sauveur de la Torchère, rue du Cherche-Midi. *Fig. d:* Rear view of fig. c. *Fig. e:* Toilette for the mother of the bride. *Fig. f:* Rear view of fig. e. *Fig. g:* Toilette for civil ceremony. *Fig. h:* Rear view of fig. g. *Fig. i:* Contract toilette. *Fig. j:* Rear view of fig. i.

*Fig. a:* Visiting dress. *Fig. b:* Rear view of fig. a. *Fig. c:* Toilette for a mature wedding guest. *Fig. d:* Rear view of fig c. *Fig. e:* Toilette for wedding guest. *Fig. f:* Rear view of fig. e. *Fig. g:* Bride's princesse-style toilette. *Fig. h:* Rear view of fig. g.

*Fig. a:* Matinee with embroidered trim. *Fig. b:* Lace fan. *Fig. c:* Tulle boudoir cap. *Fig. d:* Matinee with embroidered trim. *Fig. e:* Wrapper (dressing gown). *Fig. f:* Matinee with embroidered trim. *Fig. g:* Embroidered boudoir cap. *Fig. h:* Fan with embroidery. *Fig. i:* Bag for fan. *Fig. j:* Elegant lingerie for stout lady. *Fig. k:* Elegant trousseau lingerie.

*Fig. a:* Travel cases for toilet articles, parasols, underwear, collars and cuffs and miscellaneous items. *Figs. b–d:* Corsets, of silk or cotton jersey that girdle the waist and envelop the hips without exerting unhealthy pressure. *Figs. e–g:* Corset covers. *Fig. h:* Princesse combination. *Fig. i:* Dressing gown. *Fig. j:* Skirt and matinee.

*Fig. a:* Bridesmaid's dress. White pongee under white lace skirt, partially hidden by a draped tunic of changeable pink and brown mousseline de soie. Pink silk bows and pleated edgings. Large collar and trim of guipure. *Fig. b:* Toilette for wedding guest. Coarse yellow tulle and pale green taffeta trimmed with dark green braid. *Fig. c:* Dress for a mature lady. Green and violet glacé taffeta with a wide panel of heavy guipure. *Figs. d–f:* Rear view of figs. a–c. *Fig. g:* Contract toilette. White *météore* covered in pink mousseline de soie, under a tunic of pale blue mousseline de soie shot with silver. The front of the dress is ornamented with jeweled buttons and a silver lace collar. *Fig. h:* Rear view of fig. g.

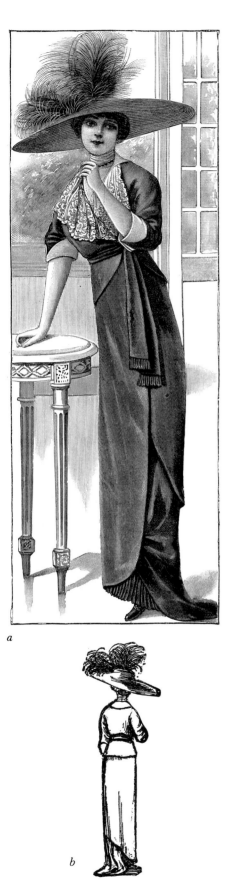

*Fig. a:* Toilette for a civil wedding. Japanese blue Liberty trimmed with mousseline de soie and antique lace. The bodice opens over a white tulle guimpe framed by antique lace revers. *Fig. b:* Rear view of fig. a. *Fig. c:* Bridesmaid's toilette. Pale blue Liberty with a flat flounce of white Venetian lace. The kimono bodice, trimmed with guipure revers and matching bib, opens over a pleated tulle plastron with low, round neck. *Fig. d:* Bride's toilette. Cream *météore* trimmed with embroidered mousseline de soie. The kimono bodice is open over a plastron of mousseline de soie pleated horizontally on the high collar and vertically below, joined by an insertion of Irish lace. An embroidered mousseline collar is square in back and forms revers in front. The bonnet-shaped veil is held by a headband of *météore* trimmed with a bouquet of flowers. *Fig. e:* Dress for mother of the bride. Gray-blue taffeta with a white lace tunic covered with black mousseline de soie. The bodice matches the tunic and is cut in kimono shape. *Figs. f–h:* Rear views of figs. c–e.

Bridal toilette by Mlles Sauveur de la Torchère, rue du Cherche-Midi.